NINJAGO™
Masters of Spinjitzu

FROM GHOSTS TO PIRATES

Story and art by Blue Ocean Entertainment AG
Additional art by Caravan Studio

L B

LITTLE, BROWN BOOKS FOR YOUNG READERS
www.lbkids.co.uk

LITTLE, BROWN BOOKS FOR YOUNG READERS

First published in the United States in 2016 by Little, Brown and Company
First published in Great Britain in 2016 by Hodder and Stoughton

1 3 5 7 9 10 8 6 4 2

Produced by Hodder and Stoughton under license from the LEGO Group.
© 2016 The LEGO Group
Comic artwork © 2016 by Blue Ocean Entertainment AG, Germany
Stories written by Christian Hector, Clemens Frey and Tine S. Norbøll
Pencils by Jon Fernandez
Inks by Ivan Solans
Colours by Oriol San Julian and Javi Chaler
Page 64 art by Caravan Studio: Hendy Setiawan & Indar Gunawan (colour).

The moral rights of the authors and illustrators have been asserted.

A CIP catalogue record for this book
is available from the British Library.

ISBN 978-1-510201-19-4

Printed in China

Little, Brown Books for Young Readers
An imprint of
Hachette Children's Group
Part of Hodder and Stoughton
Carmelite House
50 Victoria Embankment
London EC4Y 0DZ

An Hachette UK Company
www.hachette.co.uk

www.hachettechildrens.co.uk

COLE

Cole is a very calm and intelligent member of the ninja. He commands the element of Earth, giving him great physical strength and durability.

JAY

Always telling jokes, Jay is the most lighthearted of the ninja. He can harness the elements of Lightning to create a Spinjitzu tornado of pure electricity.

ZANE

Zane is the most reserved and serious of the ninja, but he is also the most respectful. His affinity for Ice allows him to freeze objects and perform a chilly Spinjitzu attack.

NYA

No one goes through a bigger change than Nya. After being told she can't go on the quest, she learns she could become the most powerful weapon against the ghosts—as the Water Ninja. But does that mean she can't be Samurai X anymore? After her initial reluctance, she'll have to learn to go with the flow.

MASTER WU

+ MISAKO

With an eye toward retirement, Master Wu and Misako have purchased a tea farm with the hope of starting a business. But when things get rough, they'll need everything, including the kitchen sink, to survive the coming days.

GHOST NINJA

It is a Season of Change...

Since defeating Master Chen and his army in the Tournament of Elements, the ninja have never been more united. Yet Lloyd mourns the loss of his father to the Cursed Realm and questions his path ahead. That's when a cold wind blows through Ninjago...

The cursed spirit of Morro—the Master of Wind, who also happens to be Master Wu's first pupil—has possessed Lloyd and seeks the Realm Crystal, and a way to help the evil Preeminent....

IN MORRO'S HIDEOUT

AT LAST I HAVE EVERYTHING I NEED TO BRING MY **MASTER** INTO THIS WORLD. BUT THESE NINJA ARE ALWAYS SPOILING MY FUN.

I'VE GOT IT. I'LL TURN THE TABLES ON THEM AND SPOIL *THEIR* FUN!

MWAHAHAHA!

OH, YES, I DEFINITELY WANT TO BE IN ON THAT!

GHOULTAR, GRAB A COUPLE OF GHOST NINJA AND GO TO THE OLD AMUSEMENT PARK. BANSHA AND WRAYTH, YOU WILL LURE THE NINJA INTO OUR TRAP!

I'LL SOON WIPE THE SMILE OFF THOSE NINJA'S FACES.

SWOOSSSH!

SWOOSSSH!

HEHEHE!

SKY PIRATES

AFTER OUR BRAVE NINJA DEFEATED THE EVIL MORRO, THE NEXT MENACE IS ALREADY LYING IN WAIT FOR THEM: SKY PIRATES! WILL THE NINJA BE ABLE TO SAVE THE WORLD YET AGAIN?

TOP NEWS

Oh, no, Morro and the Preeminent are attacking!

This cool team can handle anything!

NO MORE EVIL GHOSTS!

At last, it's over! The brave ninja have proven their skills as ghost hunters and defeated the mean Morro and his evil master. As a Master-in-Training, Lloyd learned that he can rely on his friends. Nya unlocked her full potential and defeated the ghosts with a huge wave. The only one who is still allowed to be ghostly is Cole!

A NEW MISSION!

No time to recover! The ninja may be the stars of Ninjago City, but they cannot afford to rest on their laurels. Reports have been reaching us of raids by evil pirates in sinister flying machines. Our heroes are preparing to defend Ninjago! Or are they? **Find out next.**

Nadakhan is the new villain!

THE PIRATE'S STORY

Led by the nasty Djinn Nadakhan, the pirates want to take over Ninjago City! Apparently, the Sky Pirates come from a realm called Djinjago and have only one goal: to destroy our world! If you see these dastardly airborne villains, make sure to keep a safe distance. They can't be trusted—they're pirates!

39

ZAP! ZAP! ZAP!

THIS IS THE LIFE! NOW THAT THE CURSED REALM IS DEFEATED WE CAN FINALLY KICK BACK AND RELAX!

NOT TO MENTION ALL THE FREE STUFF THAT WE'RE GETTING BECAUSE WE'RE HEROES!

YEAH, WE GOT THIS AMAZING APARTMENT... FREE INTERNET, NO RENT...

SHOULDN'T WE DO SOME NINJA TRAINING, GUYS? WE HAVEN'T PRACTICED IN DAYS.

NOT NOW, LLOYD... BEING A GHOST MAKES ME SO TIRED...

YAWN

I'M GETTING ALL THE NEW VIDEO GAMES FROM THE GAME SHOP!

AND I'M ABOUT TO BEAT YOU IN THIS ONE! TAKE THAT!

TAP! TAP! TAP!

BOOOOM!

I CAN'T BELIEVE IT! I NEVER LOSE!

BETTER BELIEVE IT, MY BLUE FRIEND!

WATCH OUT, I'M ON FIRE!

HEY, GUYS! CHECK OUT THESE TOTALLY COOL ACTION FIGURES!

I JUST WANTED TO BUY A FEW FOR MYSELF—BUT THE GIRL IN THE STORE GAVE ME AN ENTIRE BOX!

THE NINJA'S POPULARITY DOESN'T LAST LONG. SUDDENLY THEY HAVE BECOME PUBLIC ENEMY NO. 1...

BREAKING NEWS · BREA

SOMEONE HELP!

IT'S ACTUALLY NADAKHAN, THE DJINN, FRAMING THEM.

POOF!

MWHAHAHA!

SWOOOSH!

THE SIX NINJA ARE CAUGHT AND LOCKED UP IN KRYPTARIUM PRISON...

THE SHACKLES ARE MADE OF VENGESTONE. PRETTY GOOD FOR SHUTTING DOWN YOUR POWERS!

I CAN'T BELIEVE IT! WE'RE STUCK HERE, WHILE THE DJINN'S ROAMING AROUND FREE!

WE NEED TO FIND A WAY OUT OF HERE AND STOP HIM.

ACCORDING TO MY ANALYSES, THERE'S NO POSSIBLE ESCAPE.

WHAT ARE YOU DOING, JAY?

TRYING TO DIG A WAY OUT. WITHOUT MUCH LUCK, AS YOU SEE...

SO WHAT DO WE KNOW ABOUT THIS DJINN?

DID SOMEONE SAY DJINN? YOU BEST NOT BE SPEAKING ABOUT NADAKHAN THE DJINN...

HEY, IT'S CAPTAIN SOTO— THE FIRST CAPTAIN OF THE *DESTINY'S BOUNTY*!

AND IT IS JAY—THE WHINY, SNIVELLING BLUE PAJAMA MAN WHO SAYS EVERYTHING OBVIOUS.

LET'S CUT THE SMALL TALK. YOU KNOW NADAKHAN.

SURE DO. I WAS THE ONE WHO CAUGHT HIM. THE TRICK TO CATCHING A DJINN AIN'T BE GETTING HIM INTO THE VESSEL; IT'S MAKING SURE HE DON'T POOF AWAY WHILE YOU DO IT.

HA! EASY—JUST WISH HIM INTO THE TEAPOT.

EASY? PAH. EVERYONE KNOWS YOU CAN'T WISH FOR MORE WISHES, YOU CAN'T WISH FOR LOVE, AND YOU CAN'T WISH TO HARM OTHERS. WISHING A DJINN INTO A TEAPOT WOULD MOST CERTAINLY FALL INTO THAT LAST CATEGORY. TO STOP A DJINN YOU MUST...

THE LOST
SCROLLS
OF SPINJITZU

Ninjago map

1. Golden Peaks
2. Master Chen's Island
3. Ninjago City
4. Anacondrai Tomb
5. Samurai X Cave
6. Steep Wisdom Tea Farm
7. Kryptarium Prison
8. Hiroshi's Labyrinth
9. Tomb of the First Spinjitzu Master
10. Tiger Widow Island
11. Temple of Airjitzu
12. Wailing Alps
13. Corridor of Elders
14. City of Stiix
15. Spirit Coves

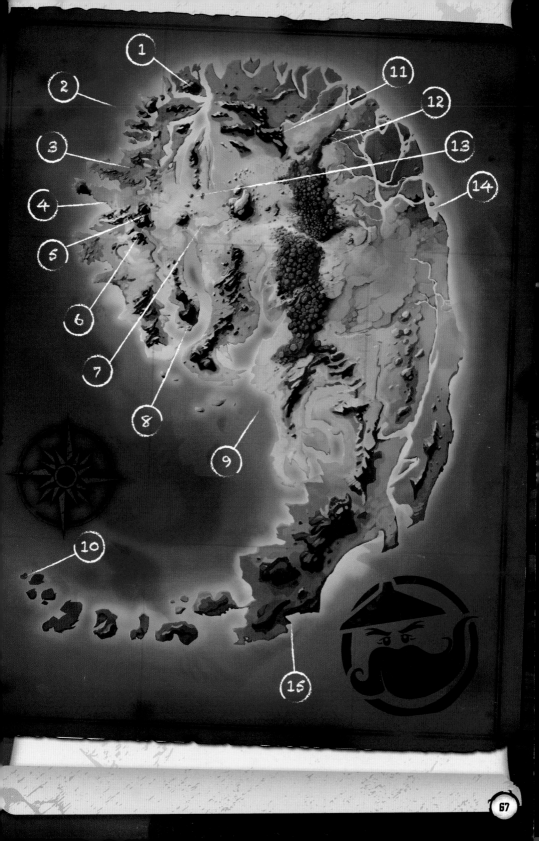

Villains

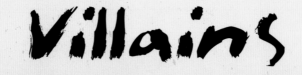

THE SKY PIRATES

Long ago, during the era of the Stone Warriors, a group of pirates dominated the high seas. Led by their Djinn captain, Nadakhan, these fierce brigands raided coastal towns and merchant ships in their ship, the *Misfortune's Keep*. The sight of their vessel struck fear into the hearts of mariners everywhere.

Finally, the *Destiny's Bounty*, commanded by Captain Soto, tracked down the *Misfortune's Keep*. In the battle that followed, Soto succeeded in defeating Nadakhan. The Djinn was trapped in the Teapot of Tyrahn. And his pirate crew was marooned in assorted other realms. There, they remained for years.

Recently, Nadakhan was unwittingly let loose. Once he was free, he sought out his old band of pirates. They refit the *Misfortune's Keep* so she could fly, and the Djinn renamed his crew the Sky Pirates.

NADAKHAN

Nadakhan is a Djinn, a magical being capable of granting wishes—although they often do not turn out the way the wisher expects. He is a prince in the royal house of Djinjago, the extra-dimensional home of his people, as well as the captain of the crew of the *Misfortune's Keep*.

Long ago, he was captured by Captain Soto and trapped in the Teapot of Tyrahn. He remained there until being freed by a ghost named Clouse. Arrogant, manipulative, and cunning, Nadakhan vowed revenge on the ninja when he discovered they were accidentally responsible for the destruction of his home realm.

Armed with the Djinn Blade, he set out to capture the ninja, marry Nya (who looked exactly like his long-lost love), build a new version of Djinjago, and gain the power to grant himself unlimited wishes.

Nadakhan is capable of granting three wishes to an individual, although he twists the words of the wishes so they never turn out as expected. Instead,

they're usually way, way worse. Those wishes cannot involve inflicting harm on another, acquiring the love of another, or requesting more wishes. If the first two wishes go badly, Nadakhan offers the opportunity to "wish it

all away," which results in the unfortunate wisher being trapped in the Djinn Blade. (And of course Nadakhan makes sure the first two wishes go badly.) Although

Nadakhan has the power to grant wishes to others, he is not able to grant his own.

CLANCEE

Clancee is a nervous, peg-legged Serpentine who occupies the lowest rung among the *Misfortune's Keep* crew. He tends to get both seasick and airsick. Clancee is the only member of the crew who never wanted to make a wish for himself, saying that he is perfectly content to live the life of a pirate. Clancee isn't too bright, but by not giving Nadakhan a chance to transform him, he may be smarter than most of his crewmates.

Weapon: Mop

Quote: "And look at me, Cap'n, I'm no longer airsick…oops, spoke too soon."

FLINTLOCKE

Flintlocke is Nadakhan's trusted first mate. For a Sky Pirate, Flintlocke has his feet on the ground. He's willing to follow his captain anywhere, as long as he has some idea where they are heading. But he expects the same loyalty back, and that will lead to trouble down the line.

Weapon: Pistol

Quote: "I'll believe that when I believe a pirate be born to tell the truth…We've sacrificed a lot to follow you, but trust is a wind that blows both ways."

DOGSHANK

The woman known as Dogshank was once someone who complained that she was always the "second prettiest" at the ball. She wanted to stand out. Nadakhan granted her wish by transforming her into a hulking brute strong enough to use an anchor and chain as a weapon. She is a powerful fighter, but has her own unique code of honor, even when fighting a ninja. She and Nya will encounter each other on a few occasions and come to enjoy their fighting "playdates."

Weapon: Ship's anchor
Quote: "We fight like girls, not like cheaters. Let's see what else you've got."

MONKEY WRETCH

Monkey Wretch is the mechanical monkey who takes care of the tech and does general repairs on the *Misfortune's Keep*. Monkey Wretch was once a regular ship's mechanic. He was skilled but wanted more and more work. Nadakhan tricked him into wishing for more hands and more speed, and then gave it to him by turning him into a mechanical monkey!

Weapon: Various tools
Quote: *"Screech!"*

DOUBLOON

Once a "two-faced thief" who tried to steal gold from Nadakhan, Doubloon is now two-faced for real. His facial expressions are on a pair of masks, so he can look happy or unhappy. Doubloon never talks, but he is an effective fighter and now a valued member of Nadakhan's crew.

Weapon: Pirate swords
Quote: Doubloon does not speak.

SQIFFY

"Sqiffy" is a new recruit to Nadakhan's crew, who signs up while the Djinn is rebuilding Djinjago. His real name is Colin, but Nadakhan didn't feel that's a real pirate's name, so he christens him Landon. When a second recruit turns out to be named Landon too, Colin's name is changed again to "Sqiffy."

Weapon: Pirate sword
Quote: Giggles while he mops.

CYREN

Cyren wanted to be the greatest singer in the world, able to enrapture audiences with her voice. Nadakhan granted her wish by making her voice capable of temporarily sending humans into a catatonic trance. It didn't do much for her career—you can't get any applause that way, and no one remembered her performance afterward—but it was a help during Sky Pirate raids. One quick tune and out went the guards...

Weapon: None. Relies on the power of her singing.
Quote: "This salt air is terrible for my voice."

BUCKD

"Bucko" is a new recruit to Nadakhan's crew. His real name is Landon, but Nadakhan changes it to Bucko.

Weapon: Pirate swords
Quote: Likes to sing while he cleans the weapons.

VEHICLES
MISFORTUNE'S KEEP

Misfortune's Keep is Nadakhan's Sky Pirate ship. After he rescues his crew from the various realms to which they have been scattered, they refit the ship so she can fly. Unbeknownst to Nadakhan, a lantern on the ship conceals Captain Soto's map to Tiger Widow Island. Jay spends a good deal of time as a captive on the ship, swabbing the decks. Later, the ninja stage an attempt to board the ship and rescue Jay. The ship is heavily armed with cannons for fighting off other vessels.

SKY SHARK

This sleek and powerful jet serves as an advance scout for the *Misfortune's Keep*. Piloted by Flintlocke, it's used to search for other ships and aircraft, and, if possible, disable them before the Sky

Pirate vessel arrives. The jet has some nasty surprises in sky battles. Two blunt anchor-shaped wings project from either side of the plane, capable of slicing through sail or steel. A hidden dynamite drop function adds an explosive punch against enemy vessels.

RAID ZEPPELIN

One of the most potent weapons in the Sky Pirates' arsenal, Raid Zeppelins are mid-sized ships held aloft by gasbags filled with hot air. The vessels are steered by ship's wheels, and armed with cannons mounted at the bow. Surprisingly maneuverable and dangerous in battle, Raid Zeppelins play an important role in the Sky Pirates' current success.

SKY GLIDERS

These one-person crafts are designed for rapid ascent, extreme maneuverability, and just enough power to bring down a larger vessel. There are many different types of Sky Gliders, all armed with different sorts of weapons. Sky Gliders work best when attacking en masse, striking like a swarm of insects against a more powerful target.

WEAPONS

DJINN BLADE

The Djinn Blade is a weapon that belongs to the royal family of Djinjago. As Djinjago collapses, Nadakhan's father, the king, gives it to Nadakhan. The Djinn Blade can trap spirits inside of it, thus providing power to the wielder. Nadakhan attempts to capture all the ninja inside the sword by manipulating them into making wishes that backfire.

VENGESTONE

A powerful substance used to make chains for prisoners. The vengestone chains binding the ninja inhibit their powers until Cole tricks Nadakhan into using magic to make them do just the opposite.

CAN YOU DECODE THE SECRET MESSAGE?

A   B   C   D   E   F   G

H   I   J   K   L   M   N

O   P   Q   R   S   T   U

V   W   X   Y   Z